History of Chicago

A Captivating Guide to the People and Events that Shaped the Windy City's History

Free Bonus from Captivating History (Available for a Limited time)

Hi History Lovers!

Now you have a chance to join our exclusive history list so you can get your first history ebook for free as well as discounts and a potential to get more history books for free! Simply visit the link below to join.

Captivatinghistory.com/ebook

Also, make sure to follow us on:

Twitter: @Captivhistory

Facebook: Captivating History:@captivatinghistory

Contents

Introduction

Chicago burst into life on the banks of Lake Michigan 200 years ago. Founded as a tiny, temporary settlement, the city became a crux of the American fur trade before growing into one of the powerhouses of the Industrial Revolution. From procuring drinking water to implementing racial equality, nothing has ever been simple for the people who have called Chicago home – and yet there is immense pride among Chicagoans for what they and their fellow people have achieved.

The city has been home to some of America's most influential people, be they talk show hosts or U.S. Presidents. Every star on the Chicago flag represents an achievement to be remembered; every building an era that has helped shape the modern city into what it is today.

Before there were deep-dish pizzas and red-hot Chicago-style hot dogs, there were simple people who fished, farmed, and lived among Native Americans who showed them how to survive. Before there were skyscrapers and the Chicago Board of Trade, there were corn, beans, cottages and weavers.

But from the minute African-descended John Baptiste Point du Sable set foot in the plains that would become one of America's greatest cities, Chicago has always been a community of well-meaning, hard-working immigrants looking for a chance to prove themselves.

Chapter 1 – The Chicago Trail of Tears

Modern Chicago is a spectacle of industry and architecture. It's a center for finance, creativity, business, and forward momentum for 10 million people in the Chicago metropolitan area, including 3 million in the city proper. When you behold this iconic American city, you inevitably see the birthplace of the skyscraper, the home of Chicago-style architecture; even the treasured adopted home of Oprah Winfrey. But long before any of these people and structures existed, Chicago was a simple tract of unspoiled prairie land next to a giant freshwater lake.

There were prairie grasses as high as a grown man's waist, spruce and poplar trees that grew thicker and thicker until they formed a vast forest, and crystalline lake waters full of fish. Ten thousand years passed on the American continents without any outside colonial influence, and it was during this time that hundreds of tribes of Bering Land Bridge migrants evolved a new set of cultures. Many Native American people hunted in the tall grass and fished in the lake, including the Sauk, Fox, Algonquin, and Miami. They bonded, fought, made camp, and moved on countless times until one tribe, the Potawatomis, took up semi-permanent residence on the land at the southwest edge of Lake Michigan.

It was the Potawatomi who inhabited the area when French explorers and settlers began to arrive in the seventeenth century. The two groups had a peaceful, or at least neutral, relationship for the first part of that century, but things changed when the New World became Europe's primary source of beaver pelts and furs. Though most European fur traders originally established a working network with members of the Huron nation, the Iroquois started attacking the Huron and any other tribes in the northwest who lay between them and the booming industry.

Unable to withstand the onslaught, the Potawatomis moved west and settled in upper Michigan and the Wisconsin forests, where they could hunt and fish in the way they were accustomed. They left the fertile land to the French, who were happy to build a settlement in the land of wild garlic, called "Chicagoua."

Eventually, the Iroquois' attacks became less frequent and different native bands were once more able to trade with Europeans. Many Potawatomi made their way back to Lake Michigan and became partners with the new residents. The natives traded furs and food items, but also took up the role of middlemen between Europeans and various tribes. They learned French and took up important roles as translators, also settling disputes whenever necessary. This was a huge asset because the Iroquois wars – known as the Beaver Wars – had upset huge numbers of Native Americans who had been forced to move, losing their lands and business prospects.

Despite the changing economy, the Potawatomi natives generally subsisted the way they always had, with hunting, gardening, and fishing. Peaceful, skilled, and willing to assist both native and European people, the tribe's territory grew larger than it had ever been in the past. The era of prosperity and expansion wouldn't last, however.

In 1789, the Potawatomi were subjected to their first land treaty, by which they procured cash and lands further west in exchange for their abandonment of the settlement on Lake Michigan. Wherever they moved, newer land treaties chased them until finally, the remaining bands were forced to become U.S. citizens or face further persecution. Though tribe members had fought with the Americans (and at other times, for the British) in the War of Independence, they were given no favors by either side. In the end, the Potawatomi tribe lost an estimated 89 million acres of pristine hunting and foraging lands, including the settlement by the Great Lake.

The surrender inspired the birth of the Citizen Potawatomi Nation, an attempt by the members of the tribe to conserve their history and culture for future generations. Today, the Citizen Potawatomi Nation is one of 39 federally recognized Native American tribes – but their headquarters are far from Chicago. A Frenchman of African descent, Jean Baptist Point du Sable, is generally credited with the foundation of Chicago as a permanent settlement at some point in the late eighteenth century.

Image Source[i]

When the last group of Potawatomi natives were driven from the area, the tribe members dressed up in full war regalia to perform a war dance. It was the last ever witnessed in Chicago.

Chapter 2 – All Roads (and Railways) Lead to Chicago

French explorers first discovered Chicago by way of the Chicago portage: a strip of land connecting the Mississippi River and the Great Lakes. Here, explorers and nomadic people would carry their canoes from one water's edge to another, thereby connecting the European-established eastern and western sections of the United States. By the mid-eighteenth century, however, things were very different from what Chicago's original inhabitants had experienced. The first step toward modernization was to make transportation as efficient and effective as possible. To that end, in 1848, both the Illinois and Michigan Canal, and the Galena and Chicago Union Railroads were completed.

Image Source[ii]

By 1837, the community was not only booming, it was incorporated as a formal city. For a decade after, it was the fastest-growing city in the United States. Originally attractive to settlers and natives as a fur trading center, the city was home to many more growing industries in the nineteenth century. With the support of its two major transportation systems, the population continued to grow as tradespeople and prospective business owners flooded in, looking for opportunities for land, jobs, and money. A few innovative people struck it rich, defining Chicago as a premier American city.

The canal ways allowed ships from the Great Lakes to connect to the Mississippi River and continue inland with cargo and passengers. Shipments of meats, produce, iron, and manufacturing tools provided Victorian Chicagoans with everything they needed to thrive, sustain families and participate in the Industrial Era that had overtaken the entire Western World. From "Annual Review of the Business of Chicago, for the year 1852:"

> The past has been a year of unexampled prosperity, and our city has shared largely in the general progress of the country. In no former year has so much been done to place its business upon a permanent basis and extend its commerce. By the extension of the Galena Railroad to Rockford, we have drawn to this city the trade of portions of Wisconsin, Iowa and Minnesota, that hitherto sought other markets; and when our roads reach the Father of Waters, as two of them will within the present year, we may expect an avalanche of business, for which we fear all our wholesale houses will not be prepared.

It wasn't just supplies and settlers who made their way to Chicago via the canals, roads, and trains; it was seasonal tourists as well. "The opening of the Rock Island Railroad, Oct. 18th to Joliet, Jan. 5th to Morris, Feb. 14th to Ottawa, and to La Salle March 10th, has brought customers during the *'lively winter'* for our businessmen (*ibid.*)"

In colder months, Chicago was visited by its northern connections who came not only to get some relief from harsh weather, but to shop. Almost simultaneous to the construction of the roads and railways, Chicago's streets grew a plethora of storefronts for a variety of products. Jewelry was an early favorite for shoppers, with just one craft house claiming to have dealt in more than $20,000 worth of decorative jewelry and watches by the end of 1852. Of course, visitors with lesser means could also fill their bags while strolling the commercial streets of the city. Chicago's many mid-eighteenth-century shops offered produce, salt, coal, pork, flour, fire-proof bricks, iron, lumber, shingles, books, furniture, dry goods, medicine, chemicals, china, glass, photography services, hardware, cutlery, banking, and insurance.

In 1865, Chicago became home to a young Marshall Field, and the commercial sector of the entire country would never be the same. After working his way through several retail positions at dry goods stores, Cooley, Wadsworth and Co., Field decided to buy into the partnership after the departure of Cooley. The company became Farwell, Field & Co. Field stayed with the general store for three years before buying into a second partnership he was offered by Levi Leiter. There were many more changes in partnership over the years, and by 1881, Marshall Field was at the head of "Marshall Field and Company."

Six years later, "Marshall Field's Wholesale Store" occupied a 4-story brick building that took up an entire city block. Built by Henry Hobson Richardson, the first department store in Chicago was one of the first three of its kind in the whole country at the end of the nineteenth century. Field's wholesale store specialized in selling bulk merchandise to small shops throughout the central and western United States; by the time he died in 1906, Marshall Field was one of the richest people in America.

The district in which the Marshall Field's store was located turned into an important commercial area of Chicago by the turn of the century – one that is still very much in vogue today. Surrounded by an elevated railway and studded with cable car turnarounds, this little piece of the city is nicknamed 'the Loop.'

Marshall Field's store wasn't just a behemoth shopping experience because of its multi-story, sprawling edifice and immense departmentalization; the fact is that Field's was a brand-new shopping experience in part because of how they were treated by staff. Workers at Field's weren't just making change and bagging items; they were there to pamper their customers. The elevator operators had even been through charm school to learn exactly how to play the role of host/hostess. What's more, the attendants at the information desk spoke several languages and happily answered questions about the store and the city. It was a plush experience that perfectly illustrated the world of nineteenth-century American capitalism and entrepreneurship.

The larger Chicago grew, the more its businesses wowed the rest of the country. Just as it had been hundreds of years previously, the settlement on the Great Lake was a hub of economic activity.

Chapter 3 – Labor and the Industrial Age

The Victorian Era was a time of huge change for the entire world, and the young city of Chicago was primed to participate to the fullest. They had a growing population, plentiful natural resources, and a well-formed infrastructure to carry them into the future. Making the move from farming and fur trading to industry seemed almost natural to a young generation of Chicagoans to whom capitalism was the glittering promise of a better future.

As in all industrializing regions, Chicagoan entrepreneurs were quick to build factories and fill them with workers. The first factory jobs were processing pork, milling wheat flour, and sawing lumber – generally making use of the supplies they had available naturally. The processed materials were not only necessary to continue feeding the residents and building more homes, but they were being bought by out-of-towners in need of the same supplies.

In 1852, two train car manufacturers were set up in Chicago. That same year, New Hydraulic Works built more than 9 miles of water pipes and completed a well, all of which were expected to soon supply the entire city with clean fresh water. Other companies in the manufacturing sector blossomed, including Mr. McCormick's reapers, wagon and carriage builders, leather tanneries, stove builders, and watch/jewelry craftsmen.

With an iron-strong infrastructure, Chicago took its next steps toward heavier manufacturing. Business owners wanted to build everything from cooking pots to bicycles, and they needed staff to churn out products in a timely manner. It was a strange time for rural families, who had always relied on farming to support themselves. Many farmers remained faithful to their farms; however, younger generations were subject to the pull of wage labor – money in exchange for hours. So, hopeful young men headed to the growing city in search of a better way of life.

Another kind of job applicant went alongside the rural people: Former slaves, recently independent thanks to the Emancipation Proclamation on January 1, 1863. Suddenly, thousands of people needed to find a place to live and work – and Chicago fit the bill perfectly. In addition to jobs and homes, Chicago offered African-Americans some of the most liberal anti-discrimination laws in the country. School and housing segregation were both outlawed by the 1880s, and though by the 1950s racial tensions had become the norm, the Industrial Revolution was a relatively beneficial time for many black people.

It was also a time of opportunity for Europeans searching for their own piece of the United States to call home. Thousands of immigrants flooded into the U.S., many staying in New York City and many others seeking out Chicago, Philadelphia, and other cities experiencing an economic boom.

STATE STREET LOOKING NORTH FROM QUINCY STREET

This immense influx of willing factory workers was beneficial for Chicago's many capitalists. Factory-processed lumber was again processed into furniture, and milled wheat was turned into bread. Chicago had become entirely self-sufficient, its gears spinning as rapidly as primary supplies and trained workers could maintain them. It seemed like there was nothing a visionary businessperson with enough investment capital couldn't achieve in the "Windy City" (more on that later.) The rest of the country – and the world – couldn't help but notice.

"Chicago," by Carl Sandburg:

"Hog Butcher for the World,

Tool Maker, Stacker of Wheat,

Player with Railroads and the Nation's Freight Handler;

Stormy, husky, brawling,

City of the Big Shoulders."

The "big shoulders" refers to Chicago's strength and importance to the rest of the United States. With money, workers, resources, and manufacturing, the city was storming into the future.

There was just one problem: working conditions – like those in every city of the Industrial Revolution – weren't sustainable. And therefore, neither was the workforce, nor the industry itself.

Tools like the drilling machine, the planer, and the metal press were incredibly dangerous and often the cause of worksite injuries and deaths. In the June 14, 1879, issue of Chicago's The Socialist, it was reported that a boiler at Bryan's Brickworks exploded, killing 5 men and injuring many more. Accidents like this were very common, and at the time, businesses lacked any kind of compensation plans for their employees. On top of that, children as young as 5 years old were regularly employed in factories alongside their family members.

With unsafe conditions, the exploitation of young children, and low wages, factory workers in Chicago were unwilling and literally unable to go on. There were a lot of labor issues to rectify, so they started with an attempt to shorten the workday. They began to talk amongst themselves and organize. After a four-year battle to instill an 8-hour maximum per day for full-time workers, laborers finally planned a strike in 1867. Sponsored by the very first Chicago Trades Assembly, the strike lasted a week and was ultimately successful.

Problems continued, however, and in 1877, a second large-scale strike occurred, this time at the railroad. These marches and protests originated in Martinsburg, West Virginia, before inciting more laborers to walk off their jobs in Philadelphia and Pittsburgh. After weeks of reading the news, Chicagoans had had enough. They took to the streets again, but this time, the protests were violent and deadly.

It wasn't just the workers from the railroad who were out marching; it was workers from the meatpacking plants and employees in the lumber mills. Chicago was incensed by class warfare between rich factory owners and poor, overworked laborers, and eventually the mostly Irish and German working class could take no more. Their grief was fueled by the local socialist group, who used the opportunity to spread its message about the rights of workers and the abuses of the ruling class – which, in this case, was capitalists.

From the 24th to the 28th of July, 1877, Chicago's streets were thick with strikers, police, socialists, and eventually military units. Though Chicagoans had already achieved the 8-hour workday in terms of legislation, employers weren't adhering to the law. Laborers and their colleagues in other cities were insistent on the regulation of their work hours, while strikers from the railways had asked for nationalization between all the stations.

On July 26th, police and the Second Militia Regiment attacked an estimated 5,000 workers at Halsted and 16th Street. Clashes between police and mostly immigrant workers were fierce, and when it was all over, at least 18 people were dead. Hundreds were wounded on all sides of the clash that was dubbed the Battle of the Viaduct.

In another conflict known as the Turner Hall Raid, police broke into a union meeting of German Furniture Workers, killing one man and wounding others. Later, the police officers were found guilty of obstructing the victims' rights to free speech.

Ultimately, the 1877 strike was fruitless for striking workers in all cities. Once order was restored to the streets, Chicago's Mayor Heath asked the factory owners to reopen immediately and "give as much employment to their workmen as possible." For the most part, employees quietly returned to work for the same wages and under the same conditions as before.

Two decades later, Chicago experienced another series of trade strikes, but these were markedly different than the ones that had come before. There were two new factors at work in the city's labor affairs by that point: the governmentally-acknowledged union and politicking. When the Chicago labor force felt it was time for another demonstration in 1894, the strike was led by the American Railway Union. The union's right to protest was recognized by the local government at first, but the immobility of many of America's railways prompted the federal court to allow the company to declare the strike illegal. After the verdict, President Grover Cleveland sent

7,000 Federal Marshals and U.S. troops into Chicago, where violence ensued once again. Even 25,000 unionists could not beat back the powers that be.

After the turn of the century, Illinois established the State Department for Factory Inspection and ceded to a 10-hour workday for women. In 1911, the Occupational Disease Act and the Workmen's Compensation Act both passed. Chicago laborers have continued to strike often in pursuit of ideal working conditions, and in 1971, the Illinois Minimum Wage Law passed.

Chapter 4 – Filthiest City in America

The Industrial Revolution created quite the dichotomy. On one hand, it gave Chicagoans jobs, goods, and connection to the rest of the world. On the other hand, the city was covered in soot, filth, and black smoke from factory chimneys for an entire century before the pollution problem was addressed. The issue came to a head in the 1950s, when workers and families started to demand better conditions for themselves and their children. From the *Chicago Tribune*:

> The smoke and soot were so thick, they blotted out the sun. Residents who hung their clean clothing to dry hauled in dingy white shirts and gritty underwear. Opened windows meant soiled curtains and filthy sills. Brand-new buildings quickly weathered as the caustic pollution ate away the stone. This isn't a dystopian vision of the future. It isn't a description of rapidly industrializing China or India. It's Chicago's past.

In addition to industrial pollution, Chicago faced the same sanitation issues as every populous city in the world: garbage, sewage, and drinking water.

In the beginning, residents drank water from Lake Michigan and put their garbage right back in it. As for wastewater, that went into the Mississippi River. For a time, these methods proved practical enough, but as the Chicago's population exploded, direct solutions for wastewater became necessary.

In 1852, the city's first sewer project was undertaken by Chief Engineer Ellis Sylvester Chesbrough. Chesbrough's plan was not particularly complex, but it was incredibly heavy-handed. The first problem he faced was that Chicago was flat and covered in the kind of dirt that turned straight to mud in the rain. Since he wanted the new sewer system to empty into the Chicago River, he'd need to create a gradient by which the water could flow. He did just that by digging earth out of the riverbed and stacking it in the parts of the city that were most congested. Chesbrough piled, installed sewers, then covered them over again. Entirely new streets had to be constructed over the completed sewers.

At the same time, Chesbrough had workers dig an intake tunnel under Lake Michigan that connected to a processing point two miles inland. In a few years' time, the sewer water had reached the mouth of Lake Michigan and begun to pollute the city's water supply. Having seen this problem solve itself during dry seasons when the flow of the river reversed, Chicago planners eventually decided to permanently reverse the Chicago River's flow. To achieve this end, public works staff had to deepen the length of the canal stretching between Bridgeport and Lockport, adding several pumps along the way. Thusly, the canal was transformed into an open sewer that merely watered down the incoming wastewater. Additionally, the intake tunnel under the lake was extended further to keep ahead of the wastewater.

By 1900, the Sanitary District of Chicago was created to deal with ongoing sewage problems. For decades, the public sewage works were entirely canal-based, and soon Chicago came under fire from its neighboring states and Canada for its proposed diversion of water from the Great Lakes. While Chicago awaited legal permission to go ahead with the diversion plan, it dug more canals. Ultimately, despite the concerns of other regions in the U.S. and Canada, Chicago achieved its goal of water diversion for the sewer.

Chicago breathed easier; neighboring St. Louis dealt with the consequences. Almost immediately, the frightening typhoid rate in Chicago plummeted by 80 percent. It was a golden era for Chicagoans, but it would only last a decade.

Ten years after the Great Lakes water diversion began flushing Chicago's sewage due southwest, the canals started to look a bit overwhelmed once more. Short on ideas, it took Chicago's administrative bodies another decade to figure out what to do about it. In the 1920s, the Supreme Court ruled to lessen the Great Lakes water diversion more and more over the course of the next 8 years, which finally motivated the city to focus on proper wastewater management instead of building more canals. In 1922, the Calumet sewage treatment works was built; more plants following in 1928, 1931 and 1939. By 1970, Chicago boasted the largest wastewater sewage system in the entire world – unfortunately, the system has never reached perfection. Even today, some Great Lakes water is still necessary to process canal overflow. Just as it was more than 100 years ago, Chicago's water treatment system is under constant pressure and surveillance.

Garbage sanitation was a whole other job. In Chicago's early days, there were dedicated quarry pits and clay pits for refuse dumping. When the city entered the industrial era, a lot more than biodegradable animal feces, food waste, paper, and natural-fiber clothing started to clog up the streets. In the 1850s, the mouth of the Chicago River started to feature a permanent collection of solid trash. The first solution to hiding all that refuse was shocking. Incredibly innovative Chief Engineer Ellis Sylvester Chesbrough needed substrate to pile on top of his new sewers, so he went ahead and used the trash.

According to the Encyclopedia of Chicago, "Many Chicago buildings and streets now rest on as much as a dozen feet of nineteenth-century refuse. The mouth of the Chicago River was transformed by landfilled refuse, and debris from the Great Fire, along with much ordinary refuse, was used to extend Lake (now Grant) Park."

During the extreme landscaping, countless piles of trash lay in the streets where residents could smell the filth and see the rats. Once the heightened landscape was sealed off with dirt, conditions improved significantly. Unfortunately, garbage collectors no longer had anywhere useful to dump the solid waste of a growing city. Furthermore, the collectors' services were inconsistent, and they tended to leave poorer neighborhoods covered in filth while attending to richer districts of the city.

"Bubbly Creek" is one example of the impact of lax garbage disposal laws. In the 1870s, meatpacking was one of Chicago's most important industries. Due to the economic importance of meat processing plants, government members and sanitation officers tended to look the other way when it came to the disposal of meatpacking waste. As usual, the natural waterways took the brunt of the problem:

> Bubbly Creek, a fork of the Chicago River, was so named because of the bubbles rising from decomposing slaughterhouse wastes. Tanneries, distilleries, and other industries dumped wastes into the North Branch of the Chicago River and the Calumet River. Iron and steel mill wastes were used to extend the lakefront of southeast Chicago and northwestern Indiana.

Thanks to the reversal of Chicago's waterways, the drinking water supply from Lake Michigan remained untouched; however, sections of the city were exposed to waste from the iron, steel, and chemical mills. Even the sewage treatment plants built in the 1920s and 1930s created sludge that wound up in the water and on the land. In the 1940s and 1950s, the advent of nuclear power created even more waste that was astoundingly used as landscape filler. During this time, advances in garbage maintenance had been made in other cities, and it was well-known how to prevent landfills from leaching dangerous toxins into the water table. Chicago, however, chose not to pursue such expensive revamps.

Instead, in the 1950s, Chicago dealt with the constant rise in garbage by choosing to incinerate most of it. Unfortunately, this solution only added to the already big issue of soot and air pollution. The city was forced to burn and bury everything, and by 1962, the city was forced to export nearly 3 million cubic yards of garbage to as many as 72 rural dumps.

The latter half of the twentieth century brought more waste than any part of the world had ever seen thanks to single-use packaging, disposable goods, and widespread commercial plastic use. By the 1980s and 1990s, fortunately, sanitary landfill processes were finally underway and only a few hundred private refuse incinerators were still in use. Illegal dumping continues to plague the city but there are many organizations in place to try to curb it and clean up the worst-polluted parts of the city.

Sanitation is an ongoing battle in what has often been called the Filthiest City in America.

Chapter 5 – The Financial District of America

Public works aside, Chicago worked hard to identify itself as a center for commerce as early as possible. The city became home to the Chicago Board of Trade in 1848, the First Chicago Bank in 1863, and the Federal Reserve Bank in 1914.

The creation of the Chicago Board of Trade was probably inevitable. Chicago's prime location among big industry sectors, coupled with the ever-impressive spider web of railroads, canals (the ones which weren't open sewers) and roads, meant that it was the perfect place for top CEOs and financial experts to gather and plan their futures. As early as the first half of the nineteenth century, that's exactly what they did.

Without a doubt, the founding of the Chicago Board of Trade was one of the most important and formative events for the city and the organization of U.S. finance as a whole. This organization came into being to help buyers and sellers of commodities – two groups who were not in short supply in the hub that was Chicago – protect their investments. It was one of the first futures and options exchanges in the entire world, and it's still an entity under the umbrella brand CME Group today.

The formation of the original CBOT was simple at heart. Producers of commodities like wheat and corn knew that their product was in high enough demand for them to work toward producing more – but in doing so, farmers made it impossible for themselves to grow or produce any other type of commodity. If corn took a dive the next year, they'd lose everything. They wanted security in knowing that their product was guaranteed to sell.

On the other side of the transaction, wholesale consumers of commodities wanted the security of knowing how much stock they would be able to have, and when it was coming.

The answer, as early Chicagoans saw it, was to establish a futures contract between producers and consumers. Therefore, before so much as a bushel of corn was grown, the farmer's expected output was pre-contracted to specific buyers for a predetermined price. In today's market, futures contracts like these are usually referred to as "derivatives."

The formation of the Chicago Board of Trade didn't just affect buyers and sellers in and around Chicago; it attracted American businesspeople from all over the country. Soon, every major industry in America was represented in Chicago: roads, railroads, wagons, horses, cotton, cereals, leather, ship-building, butter, eggs, meat, textiles, and factory machine parts.

With so many different types of commodities and varied buyers, the CBOT had a big responsibility to maintain quality transactions. That's why, in 1864, they created a standardized futures contract to be used in their organization.

In time, some members of the agricultural sector created their own sub-group of the CBOT, calling themselves the Chicago Butter and Egg Board. Founded in 1898, the Butter and Egg Board became the Chicago Mercantile Exchange in the twentieth century, eventually joining back up with the CBOT and forming the CME Group. Before it was taken back into the CBOT fold, the Butter and Egg Board became the primary organization for agricultural sellers and buyers to put together their specialized futures contracts.

In addition to futures, agricultural producers and wholesale buyers started to create "options" contracts amongst themselves. With an option contract between two parties, the buyer or the seller is given the right to buy or sell a commodity at a specific price and by a specific date. An egg producer and the head of a grocery outlet, for example, might agree that if the grocery outlet buys eggs before September, he can buy them for the reduced price of 50 cents per crate.

Trade in Chicago boomed, cementing the direction in which the entire country was headed. Primary commodity production rose; secondary manufacturing continued to evolve in complex ways, and the end-consumer was privy to more products than at any other point in history.

Having consolidated its reputation as a vital cog in the machine that was America, Chicago set up its first banking center 15 years after the CBOT was established. Edmund Aiken and other investors used $100,000 to start the company in 1863. Federally registered as Charter Bank #8, First Chicago Bank played an important role in stabilizing Chicago during and after the American Civil War.

When the Union and the Confederate Armies were at war from 1861 to 1865, Chicago found itself far enough from the front lines to continue manufacturing and shipping goods with little disruption. Unfortunately for other cities like St. Louis and Cincinnati, their adjacent railways and Mississippi River trade routes were often too close to the fighting to be used. Chicago's factories and laborers picked up the slack, supplying the Union Army with goods, supplies, and transportation to continue Abraham Lincoln's fight for American unity.

Chicago wasn't the only supplier of the Union Army, or even the most important, but it was still a strategic center. The city provided millions of dollars' worth of horses, meat, tents, harnesses, hardtack, and other items to the U.S. Army before the end of the war.

While racial tensions ran high in Chicago as in other cities in the United States, Chicago provided some stability to residents and visitors during the Civil War. The establishment of the First Chicago Bank was so important to area residents who relied on bank transactions to run their businesses and pay their bills that by the end of the Civil War, there were a total of thirteen national banks located there. That was more than any other city in the country.

Following the Civil War, Chicago's factory industry and population had tripled. The city had taken over from St. Louis as the main pork provider for the country, and banking and finance had become just as important to the city as its manufacturing sector.

The original First Chicago Bank chain still operates today under the brand First Chicago. In 1914, the Federal Reserve Bank was built in Chicago. It is still one of America's 12 reserve banks that make up the country's central bank today. Responsible for overseeing the local economy as well as offering regular banking services like payment processing and cash withdrawal, the Federal Reserve Bank employs roughly 1,600 people. It is a staple in the city's banking sector just as it was a century ago.

Today, Chicago's economy ranks about 21st in size when compared to the rest of the world. Its financial sector is ranked the third most competitive in the United States (behind New York City and San Francisco) and the seventh most competitive in the world. Its financial economy is still heavily based on the CME Group, plus the Chicago Stock Exchange, the Chicago Board Options Exchange, NYSE Arca, and many brokerage and insurance companies.

The rest of the city's economy rests on the shoulders of the transportation industry, government services, manufacturing, printing, and food production – all built on the foundation laid by nineteenth-century shopkeepers, farmers, commercial leaders and railway builders.

Chapter 6 – Workers' Cottage to Skyscraper; Chicago's Architecture and Design

While the factory owners were turning Chicago into a capitalist's dream and the banks and trade organizations were stabilizing local industries, the architects got to work transforming the cityscape. From "Annual Review of the Business of Chicago, for the year 1852," "Elegant residences have been built in all parts of the city, splendid blocks of stores have been erected on our principal streets, and the limits of the inhabited part of the city have been greatly extended."

Just like the railroad, the canals and the manufacturing sector had their beginnings in 1852 – so too did Chicago's major architectural themes.

If the lavish commercialism of the mid-nineteenth century wasn't enough to draw the Victorian crowds to Chicago, the beautiful homes did the trick. All the money flowing into the city during the industrial era didn't just bring bulk commodities into Chicago; money was being spent on pristine homes for the city's nouveau-riche. Three-story and four-story houses lined residential streets after the 1850s, replacing the quaint, boxy workers' cottages that had been popular in preceding decades. These were architecturally advanced, highly-detailed, and communicative of a reasonable amount of opulence. They heralded the success and business acumen of the city's business owners.

Before there was wealth, however, there was the worker's cottage. These were what you would have found in Victorian Chicago as the factories were still taking root, while freed slaves and European immigrants found their way to the city in droves.

The humble worker's cottage generally featured a classic A-roof (half-gabled) facing the street, a raised basement and a long, skinny body to fit the classic Chicago land lot. They had two stories, 2-4 bedrooms, a parlor, kitchen, and pantry area. There was a separate outhouse built outside.

The Loop was outfitted with these kinds of houses, usually built by the owners. Cottages tended to be wood before 1871, and brick afterward. Though these simple family homes are a huge part of

Chicago's past, today you'll find only a few of them dotting residential streets such as Lincoln Park, the Lower West Side, and West Town. There are two reasons for that. The first is due to fire, and the second is due to modern builders knocking them down.

Unfortunately, the Great Chicago Fire of 1871 wiped out much of the city's Victorian and Civil War-era downtown buildings, but the creative energy with which the city rebuilt itself is something we can see in the post-Great Fire buildings that still exist today. Cottages were still built by middle-class workers, but these were surpassed by townhouses and Chicago's famous Greystone homes.

Greystones were a marvel of beauty, function, and true Chicago ingenuity. The limestones themselves were quarried directly in Illinois, which made the buildings affordable and efficient. The classic Roman style of those first Greystones – built generally between 1890 and 1930 – belied a changing attitude in the contemporary Chicagoan – one of art, intellect, and means. These gorgeous homes possessed recessed windows, columns and arches in a variety of designs.

Though the basic style of Chicago's homes evolved through the decades, the Greystone itself remained popular with builders and home buyers alike. Even now, Greystones with Roman style, Chateau-style, or Queen Anne-style architecture are preserved and presented proudly by owners and preservation organizations.

No retelling of Chicago's love affair with architectural design would be complete without mentioning Frank Lloyd Wright, one of the most famous American building designers to have had a hand in Chicago's ongoing creation.

Wright arrived in Chicago in the late 1880s, not quite two decades after the Great Chicago Fire destroyed most of the downtown section of the city. It was the perfect environment for a man of his talents and drive. Wright came to the city looking for work; it's safe to say he found enough to occupy his time.

When the would-be prodigy from Wisconsin first came to Chicago, he was not impressed by the things he saw around him. He thought the city was dirty and grim, but full of possibilities. After finding employment as a draftsman for Joseph Silbee, Wright learned the foundations of his new career and found himself upwardly mobile in the local industry. As he developed his own design style, the "organic" and "Prairie School" concepts became a part of his signature drawings and concepts, though the latter term was not used by the architect himself.

Wright and his architectural followers (such as Marion Mahoney Griffin, Walter Burley Griffin and Trost & Trost) designed homes with two easy-to-spot features, such as overhanging eaves and bold horizontal lines. Hence the term "prairie" in the stylistic description. Aficionados and historians saw these horizontal expanses as an echo of the original rolling, flat plains that occupied Chicago and other Midwestern cities before urbanization. Wright, though he called the style "organic," was in agreement.

Frank Lloyd Wright's name is pretty much synonymous with twentieth-century American housing, with good reason. He built 500 homes, schools, churches and public spectacles like the Guggenheim Museum, but it is the homes and the overall style that really became part of Chicago for the long haul.

As the man himself said, "Eventually, I think Chicago will be the most beautiful great city left in the world."

While Wright and his colleagues gave the middle-class Chicagoan a new choice in home design, William Le Baron Jenney was making architectural inroads of his own – most significantly, the Home Insurance Building at the corner of LaSalle and Adams Streets.

Le Baron Jenney's most influential innovation wasn't just height; it was the use of metal in place of stone. Since Chicago was already wood-shy in the aftermath of the Great Fire, architects at the end of the nineteenth century generally favored stone building materials. Though stunning and versatile, the immense weight of building stones didn't allow for much height. When metal support beams entered the picture, a squat office building could suddenly be heightened by several stories. So, that's exactly how Le Baron Jenney proceeded. When the Home Insurance building was finished, it stood ten stories tall, framed in steel and covered in stone. It was fire-resistant, gravity-resistant, and at 138 feet, it was the tallest commercial building in the world.

Image Source[xii]

Ultimately, the first skyscraper was demolished in 1930 to make way for the brand-new Field Building (also known as the LaSalle National Bank Building.) As it was broken down and carted away, Le Baron Jenney's masterpiece was carefully studied by teams of architects and designers who were keen to cement the building's reputation as the world's first skyscraper. Marshall Field himself appointed a committee to look into the status of the building he was tearing down. According to that committee's report:

> We have no hesitation in stating that the Home Insurance building was the first high structure to utilize as its basic principle of its design the method known as skeleton construction and that there is much evidence that William Le Baron Jenney, the architect, in solving the particular problems of height and loads appearing in this building, discovered the true application of skeleton construction in the building of high structures and invented and here utilized for the first time its

special forms. We are also of the opinion that owing to its priority and its immediate success and renown the Home Insurance building was in fact the primal influence of skeleton construction, the true father of the modern skyscraper.

Chapter 7 – 1860 Republican National Convention

May 16-18, 1860

Chicago in 1860 was a city of immigrants, second-generation immigrants, capitalists, and laborers. Factory workers were heavily influenced by the local Communist Party because of the latter's support of trade unions and worker strikes. The Whig Party had just disbanded, and the Democratic Party of the United States had become too centrist for a population of Americans who largely supported the abolishment of slavery. Fresh on the scene was the Republican Party – and the electorate was so invested in the outcome of the 1860 convention that Chicago literally couldn't house all the attendees under one roof. Officials built a temporary wooden structure – named the Wigwam – to seat 10,000 Republican delegates and guests. No Southern states sent delegates.

The Wigwam was commissioned by multiple Chicago businesses who specifically wanted to appeal to the Republicans and host them during the convention. It was constructed at Lake and Wacker, and it stood for as long as a decade afterwards. During the impending Civil War, the Wigwam (a Native American word used to refer to a temporary shelter) was used for political and strategy meetings. In 2002, the spot on which the original wigwam stood was designated a Chicago Landmark.

THE REPUBLICANS IN NOMINATING CONVENTION IN THEIR WIGWAM AT CHICAGO, MAY, 1860.

Image Source[xiii]

The 1860 Republican Platform was mainly based on the highly-controversial issue of slavery. Though the newly-formed Republican Party was something of a conglomerate of single-issue and fringe parties, each member firmly believed not only in the abolition of Southern slavery, but the establishment of "Free Soil" and gentle fugitive slave legislation throughout the United States.

Free Soilers were focused on keeping slavery out of states in which black people were already free; this was an important issue brought forward by a number of new Republicans who had originally formed their own political party. A number of anti-slavery declarations were listed on the official platform document, but there were unrelated declarations as well. Among these were the stated necessity for including Kansas in the Union, higher wages for workers and farmers, and the provision of free homesteads for pre-screened settlers.

When the platform was read out to delegates and guests at the Republican Convention, it was met with thunderous applause and immediately accepted by unanimous vote.

Afterward, the convention focused on the major task at hand: selecting their candidate for President of the United States. From The Washington Times:

> William H. Seward, the Republican front-runner from New York, sent his political team to Chicago to lock up his party's nomination. In the mid-nineteenth century, it was not considered proper for the aspiring candidate to go to the convention himself, so Seward sent his political manager, Thurlow Weed, along with his states' 70 delegates and 13 railroad cars of supporters.

Abraham Lincoln ran his own Presidential campaign regardless of the odds, and according to historian Gordon Leidner, his team performed all kinds of stunts to help their candidate win:

> Lincoln's men left no detail unattended in their pursuit of this strategy. They made certain that Seward's New Yorkers were seated far from other critical delegations with whom they might collaborate. They printed hundreds of counterfeit tickets and distributed them to Lincoln supporters with instructions to show up early--in order to displace Seward's supporters. They also assigned two men with noted stentorian voices to lead the cheering. One of these men reportedly had a larynx powerful enough to allow his shout to be heard across Lake Michigan.

When William Seward's delegation belatedly reached the convention on the third and final day, they found that their seats had been taken by the counterfeited Lincoln-supporter tickets. Nevertheless, the frontrunner did well through several rounds of voting, advancing until he and Lincoln were head-to-head.

The Republicans knew that the presidential candidate from the Democratic Party was Stephen A. Douglas, an Illinois-born politician with huge Chicago support. As another son of Illinois, Abraham Lincoln also enjoyed popularity in the convention city. When his campaign gained momentum in leaps and bounds just as planned, the rest of the convened Republicans began to consider the benefits of pitting Lincoln against Douglas directly. The two had previously battled one another for the state governorship two years earlier, with Douglas coming out as the winner.

On the third ballot, Lincoln was just one and one-half votes short of having achieved the nomination. In a shaky, stuttering voice, the delegate from Ohio stood and made an announcement that changed the way in which the future would unfold: four votes were amended and redistributed to Lincoln.

Image Source[xiv]

Of course, winning the nomination at the Republican Convention in Chicago was just the first step toward the presidency, but ultimately, Abraham Lincoln won that as well. He appointed William Seward his Secretary of State and saw the Union through a Civil War that eventually led to the nationwide abolishment of slavery – the exact reason for which the Republican Party was formed.

A few months later, after winning the presidential election, Lincoln faced an overwhelming crowd of journalists outside the porch of his home in Springfield, Illinois. Unwilling to give them much of his time, the President-elect spoke for only a brief few minutes. In doing so, he reignited the excitement of the country that had voted for his leadership. "Let us at all times remember that all American citizens are brothers of a common country, and should dwell together in the bonds of fraternal feeling."

Chapter 8 – World's Columbian Exposition in Chicago

It was the 400th anniversary of Christopher Columbus' arrival in the New World, and Americans wanted to celebrate. At least, their government wanted them to.

1893 was a strange year for many people in Chicago. The Great Fire was still present in their memories and the streets; the Civil War was an even closer memory. The Industrial Revolution was in full swing while the Reconstruction of the country petered out into the Gilded Age. People were confused about their place in the world and even in neighboring states. African Americans were crowding into the workplace while many whites still tried to dominate them.

Americans needed a dose of unity, and Congress ultimately decided to give it to them. Though other cities, including New York City, put in strong bids to become hosts, Chicago was the winner for financial and logistical reasons.

Many rich Chicagoans helped to finance the World's Fair, including steel manufacturer Charles H. Schwab, iron magnate Milo Barnum Richardson, and banker Lyman Gage. It was Gage who finally persuaded Congress to award his city with the project thanks to last-minute fundraising that beat out New York City's bid. In addition to the million pledged to the event if Chicago played host, the city was also able to provide the open square-footage necessary to receive hundreds of thousands of people and build immense temporary structures.

Jackson Park was chosen for the exhibition, and the offices for the event were located on Adams Street in the Rand McNally Building. Architect Daniel Burnham was made director; working closely with a small team, he decided to construct an ideal cityscape according to the principles of *Beaux Artes*.

Imported from France, the *Beaux Artes* style was largely neoclassicist. It was featured at the 1889 Paris Universal Exposition, an international event that heavily influenced Burnham's own design for the Chicago Fair. "Make no little plans," Burnham said. "They have no magic to stir men's blood. Make big plans, aim high in hope and work and let your watchword be order and your beacon beauty."

His designs for the Columbian Exposition were impeccable and detailed. In all, the fairgrounds covered over 600 acres of land. There were pavilions to represent 46 nations, a carnival midway, a 264-foot Ferris wheel, reproductions of the Niña, the Pinta, and Santa Maria (built by the U.S. and Spain) and a rudimentary movie theater. A moving platform looped around the grounds, transporting people throughout the fair.

PLATE 105

FERRIS WHEEL —FROM THE WEST

Image Source[xv]

The international community had a huge hand in building the spectacle, which was a unique part of Chicago's event. This was the first time other nations had been invited to participate via the national pavilions. Norway sent a classic ship called the Viking, which currently resides in Geneva, Illinois. A German company set up an artillery exhibition that ironically showcased guns which were the precursors to World War I howitzers.

The main structures of the little city were coated in white stucco and the streets were lit brightly with electric lights, giving the entire exhibition a happy glow. It was dubbed the "White City."

Image Source[xvi]

Part of the administrative design of the international pavilions at the fair involved each nation appointing its own delegate. The Haitian pavilion chose Frederick Douglass as its representative. This proved to be a controversial move, given that Douglass was one of the most prominent ex-slaves of the day.

Douglass teamed up with several prominent African-Americans to co-author a pamphlet entitled "The Reason Why the Colored American Is Not in the World's Columbian Exposition." The authors were well-founded in their frustration and anger, given that very few African American people were given jobs or allowed to have their own exhibitions at the event. Zero people of color were allowed to take up the role of exhibition police guard. "Theoretically open to all Americans, the Exposition practically is, literally and figuratively, a 'White City,' in the building of which the Colored American was allowed no helping hand, and in its glorious success he has no share. It remained for the Republic of Hayti [sic] to give the only acceptable representation enjoyed by us in the Fair."

The authors lamented that their people had not been given a chance to celebrate, work with their neighbors and take pride in their achievements.

The enthusiasm for the work which permeated every phase of our National life, especially inspired the colored people who saw in this great event their first opportunity to show what freedom and citizenship can do for a slave. Less than thirty years have elapsed since 'Grim visaged war smoothed its wrinkled front,' and left as a heritage of its short but eventful existence four millions of freedmen, now the Nation's wards. In its accounting to the world, none felt more keenly than the colored man, that America could not omit from the record the status of the former slave. He hoped that the American people with their never-failing protestation of justice and fair play, would gladly respond to this call, and side by side with the magnificence of its industry, intelligence and wealth give evidence of its broad charity and splendid humane impulses.

He recognized that during the twenty-five years past the United States in the field of politics and economics has had a work peculiar to itself. He knew that achievements of his country would interest the world, since no event of the century occurred in the life of any nation, of greater importance than the freedom and enfranchisement of the American slaves. He was anxious to respond to this interest by showing to the world, not only what America has done for the Negro, but what the Negro has done for himself.

Though the country's second World's Fair in Philadelphia had been something of a flop, Chicago's Fair was a huge success. An estimated 26 million people came to see the sights between May and October 1893, and some of the structures built for the exhibition remain to this day.

Sadly, the World's Columbian Exhibition came to a close not with celebratory closing ceremonies but with the memorial service of Chicago Mayor Carter Harrison, Sr.

The fair closed for good on October 30, 1893, and the exhibition grounds were once more a public park.

Chapter 9 – The Speakeasy and Al Capone

Like the rest of the United States, Chicago was heavily influenced by the temperance movement of the mid-nineteenth century. Big names like P.T. Barnum and Susan B. Anthony supported the philosophy that alcohol abuse was the root cause of most evils in their country. Temperance advocates rallied for prohibition in droves before legislation gave them what they wanted.

Throughout the 1850s, there were a total of 13 U.S. states that voted to ban sales of alcohol. Illinois was not one of them. Unfortunately for those involved in the movement, the American Civil War turned everything on its head. Liquor sales funded both the Union and Confederate Armies, and as long as the country was focused on the war, there was no time to discuss further prohibition in remaining states or as a federal initiative. Temperance, though still a very strong part of American culture in the latter part of the nineteenth and early twentieth century, was not included in reformative planning.

When the United States joined its allies in the First World War, the perfect opportunity presented itself to President Woodrow Wilson. To support the war effort and preserve grain for food production only, the President temporarily banned manufacturing and sales of alcohol throughout the entire country.

As the war wound down to its final conclusion, fewer and fewer American troops were sent overseas into conflict zones. Wilson saw this as evidence that the ban was no longer necessary. From The

Literary Digest, May 21, 1919: "The demobilization of the military forces of the country has progressed to such a point that it seems to me entirely safe now to remove the ban upon the manufacture and sale of wines and beers."

Not everyone was happy about the repeal. Despite Woodrow's veto, the nationalization of prohibition was ultimately passed as the Eighteenth Amendment of the United States Constitution in 1918. The law came into effect on the January, 17, 1920. The ban lasted for 13 years, ushering in the age of the speakeasy.

Three years later, a New Yorker named Alphonse Gabriel Capone bought a house in Chicago's Park Manor neighborhood. Originally a member of the New York City Five Points gang, Capone sought out a similar position in his new city. He started work with local crime boss Big Jim Colosimo, directly under his recruiter, Johnny Torrio. The same year, Colosimo was murdered. Torrio and Capone worked closely for the next five years until Torrio was shot dead, presumably by a rival gang member.

Image Source[xvii]

After 1925, the business of Colosimo/Torrio's gang fell to Capone; it was huge break for the gangster that would eventually earn him millions of dollars a year. The business-focused almost on every perceived vice of the temperance crowd: bootlegged liquor, prostitution, and gambling. Capone's gang covered Chicago's South Side, a section of the city that housed his many brothels, casinos, and speakeasies. His most lucrative property was the Four Deuces, an establishment in which customers could procure both prostitutes and alcoholic beverages. The business stood at 2222 South Wabash Avenue, South Loop.

At first, Al Capone had an excellent reputation among his fellow Chicagoans, particularly those of Italian descent. Born of Italian immigrant parents, Capone was compelled for one reason or another to spearhead a children's milk program and provide free food and drink to Chicago's unemployed and homeless. He opened several soup kitchens, and many people considered him a community leader in the 1920s and 1930s. Some even praised him for providing work to otherwise jobless Chicagoans via the bootleg liquor trade.

In fact, it was the very act of smuggling liquor over the Canadian/American border during Prohibition that gave us the term "bootleg." Smugglers regularly put bottles in their boots to cross into the United States, removing them once safely at home or in the company of friends or colleagues. The industry, also often referred to as "rum running," was heavily supplied from Canadian smuggling, but it was also fed from homemade liquors – so-called bathtub gin and moonshine.

Regardless of his reputation, it's true that Al Capone headed one of America's largest, most successful alcohol businesses under Prohibition. It's also true that he was personally connected to the murders of hundreds of people throughout his gang's territory. The highest numbers of dead come from bombings of Chicago establishments that reportedly refused to sell Capone's products. Though there were plenty of restaurants, coffee shops, and other businesses eager to put liquor back on the menu, Capone and his gang weren't satisfied with them. Every potential client either sold or was bullied into selling Capone's product, or they paid the ultimate price.

The bloodiest chapter of Capone's Prohibition-era occurred on February 14, 1929. That day, seven members of Chicago's North Side Gang were rounded up, led down a street in Lincoln Park, and shot dead with Thompson submachine guns. The hit, attributed to Capone's competing gang, was most likely meant to take out the North Side leader, George "Bugs" Moran. Moran wasn't harmed, but a known lookalike, Albert Weinshank, was killed instead.

Leading up to the massacre, Moran had taken over some of Capone's saloons and was purportedly eyeing one of his rival's dog-tracks. On top of the disregard for gang boundaries, the North Side Gang was responsible for numerous kidnappings and murders of people associated with Capone and his Chicago Outfit. No charges could stick to Al Capone, however, since he was in Florida at the time.

The murders shocked Chicago and the rest of the United States. Drinkers who had previously believed bootlegging was a harmless industry were forced to reconsider the true cost of their beer and whiskey. According to the Chicago Tribune, "These murders went out of the comprehension of a civilized city. The butchering of seven men by open daylight raises this question for Chicago: Is it helpless?"

In 1931, Capone was finally arrested after a long-winded tax evasion case. He was sentenced to eleven years in prison, of which he served six and a half, first in Atlanta and then in San Francisco's famous Alcatraz. The crime boss died at home in Palm Island in 1947, his wife by his side.

Chapter 10 – Real Chicago Flavor

The Potawatomis' food culture was complex and well-established. Tribespeople hunted deer and elk, water birds, and freshwater fish like whitefish, bass, and lake trout. They gathered wild rice and farmed corn, squash, and beans, and even tapped maple trees for their sweet sap. When Chicago was still a pristine piece of green prairie land next to the sparkling Great Lakes, people ate extremely well. Their recipes were based on what they called the Three Sisters: corn, squash, and beans.

Friendly natives showed their European counterparts how to make use of all these food sources, but settlers in the area preferred to use the ingredients differently. French immigrants craved butter and cream with their vegetables and fish, as did later generations of Eastern and Western European settlers by the lake. They wanted wheat bread, cheese, and a different variety of meats that included beef and pork. As settlers became more comfortable in their new environment, they learned how to raise and farm these familiar foods, thereby changing the culinary landscape of the Chicago region.

By the time the Native Americans were driven from the area by a succession of treaties, French, English, Irish, German, and other ethnic groups had become reliant on a mixture of local and imported foods. It was the imported foods – particularly pork, beef, and wheat – that would become the most important commodities during the Industrial Revolution.

Another non-local ingredient came into fashion after the 1830s, a time during which many New England Americans came into Chicago for jobs and business opportunities. They brought with them a love of East Coast oysters. The new seafood, imported from New England, became so popular that a brand-new eatery came onto the scene: the oyster saloon. Chicago foodies still remember this unusual part of the city's history, and today you can find modern oyster bars that hearken back to the early nineteenth century-style.

Image Source[xviii]

At the same time, Irish immigrants were pouring into Chicago to escape hard times at home, and they were looking for something familiar to eat. They had no problem finding the now-ubiquitous potato, but pickled pork was tough to come by and considerably expensive. Since beef was the preferred meat in Chicago, Irish innovators took a leap and created corned beef. It was a hit, taking off in quick-stop lunch eateries that served it with cabbage, just the way customers liked it.

An interesting component of this story is that, since Irish and Jewish immigrants tended to occupy the same neighborhoods in their adopted city, both developed a strong fondness for corned beef and a range of deli-style meats. Beef was the delicacy of the time, considered by American foodies to be the very best quality. The steakhouse reigned supreme in nineteenth-century Chicago, more so even than the delis and oyster depots that also play an important role in today's regional cuisine. Beef was not just a staple protein in large supply; it was something that rural ranchers surrounding the city raised themselves. It was a meat that thousands of factory workers processed on a daily basis. It was an ingredient that could be cured and prepared in a dozen ways, all of which could satisfy the hunger of the poorest or richest table of diners.

According to the *Encyclopedia of Chicago,* the classic steakhouse defines – and *still* defines – what Chicago food is at its heart: a collection of hearty staples to fill the belly and relax the soul. Still today, in a city with access to ingredients from anywhere on the planet, the most beloved dinner away from home is the same as it was 170 years ago: "Abundant quantities of red meat, red wine, baked potatoes, creamed vegetables, brandy, and cigars."

In the 1850s, German immigrants introduced their new neighbors to a love of sausages. Pork manufacturing was on the rise, and hot dogs came onto the scene. Vendors with carts suddenly became a constant fixture of the Chicago street corner, something that wouldn't shock a modern Chicagoan. Beer gardens came along with the German beer and bratwursts, adding a relaxed outdoor option for people who were otherwise cooped up in saloons with their drinks.

At the end of nineteenth century, Chicago became famous for its cafeteria-style dining establishments, particularly because there were no waiters to tip. Waitstaff were usually African American or Irish, two social classes who found themselves occupying the lowest-paid jobs in America. Their reputations were not helped by work in the foodservice industry, unfortunately, since the general belief of the diners was that lower-class waitstaff treated you terribly unless you over-tipped. Contrary to today, women were not often employed as waitresses, as that didn't come to be until several decades later.

Fine dining, though available as early as the 1830s, didn't really take off until the more decadent 1920s. By this point, tables were covered with cloths, menus were printed carefully on cards, and diners took care to dress properly when visiting a restaurant. An evolving palette demanded more exotic flavors, and contemporary commercial kitchens prided themselves on employing Indian or Chinese chefs. French food made a comeback for a few decades, then quickly lost its appeal to a city of modernists who found it stuffy and old-fashioned.

Two specialty foods developed in the twentieth century that Chicago would become internationally known for: the deep-dish pizza and Chicago-style hot dogs.

If you'd asked anyone in the 1850s what food item would last well into the twenty-first century, it's difficult to imagine the answer would have been "the hot dog." Nevertheless, the Chicago-style hot dog is a favorite of Chicagoans and tourists alike. Also known as a red-hot, these beef hot dogs are cradled in a poppyseed-seed bun and piled high with mustard, chopped onions, sweet pickle relish, a dill pickle slice, tomatoes, short peppers, and celery salt. Against every natural instinct possessed by the rest of America, red-hots are ketchup-free!

As for the Chicago deep-dish pizza, it has its origins in the 1940s and 1950s. No one can agree who made the very first, but top contenders are Ike Sewell and Rudy Malnati. Deep-dish delivers just what it promises, featuring a high edge that gives pizza makers two to three extra inches of space in which to pile cheese, tomato sauce, and other toppings.

Image Source[xxi]

It goes against everything an Italian holds sacred, and yet it's a movement that has caught on.

Chapter 11 – The Great Depression and Legislated Segregation

Chicago was a strong city, but it wasn't immune to the stock market crash of 1929. First, the London Stock Market crashed in September following the arrest of several top investors. Wall Street's own crash came no more than a month later, crippling the country and most of the Western world.

Many factors contributed to the economic disaster, including the almost unbridled economic success of the previous decade. America boomed in the Roaring Twenties, and Chicago was no small part of that era. Manufacturing was at an all-time high; goods were plentiful and affordable. Electricity transformed urban centers with light and air conditioning, extending the work day and earning CEOs more money. In the fields, farmers had an almost too-productive season, turning out so much wheat that the price crumbled alongside the Dow Jones.

The NYSE and the Chicago Mercantile Exchange collaborated, implementing a system in which exchange would be stopped for a period of one or two hours if the Dow Jones average fell more than 250 or 400 points. The stoppages were intended to allow traders and brokers time to re-evaluate their strategies and get in contact with clients – though the plan was criticized for inducing panic when the points started to dip.

Image Source[xxii]

Despite desperate attempts by America's wealthy to keep the stock prices from plummeting, grand and showy investment designed to demonstrate faith in the market ultimately failed. More Americans than ever had invested their money in the market during the twenties, motivated by soaring stock values that seemed endless. Unfortunately, most of them were borrowing up to two-thirds of the cost to invest. When the crash came, the United States had lent more money than it actually had in circulation. Billions of middle-class dollars were lost, and unemployment swept the nation.

In Chicago, Democrat Edward Kelly became mayor in 1933 by organizing a general coalition that was largely Irish, working-class laborers, and black men. Overjoyed to have one of the country's most powerful cities back in the hands of his own political party,

President Franklin D. Roosevelt was liberal with federal funds under an initiative called the New Deal.

The New Deal was designed to redistribute federal money to ailing cities like Chicago with specific programs that provided jobs for residents and funds for civil services. Not only would the money ease Chicago's financial troubles, but it would foster Democratic loyalty in the city's voters. This was especially unprecedented in terms of African American voters, who were virtually all Republican supporters before the stock market crash. Chicago voted Democrat overwhelmingly throughout the 1930s; it also finished construction on Lake Shore Drive, several parks, thirty schools, and a modern subway system.

Though Roosevelt's administration – and Kelly's, by association – was considered thoroughly modern and liberal at the time, it was responsible for the formation of an era of racial segregation. The Federal Housing Association came into effect in 1934, ostensibly using federal funds to create new housing for the country's many homeless. It did just that, except the fine print of the FHA legislation indicated that the new homes were not to be sold to African Americans. There was even an ownership clause that restricted resale to someone of color. Furthermore, black Americans were denied mortgage insurance.

American historian Richard Rothstein concludes that this housing segregation was completely blatant; it was written plainly in the housing manuals given to developers and salespeople:

> The Federal Housing Administration's justification was that if African-Americans bought homes in these suburbs, or even if they bought homes near these suburbs, the property values of the homes that they were insuring – the white homes that they were insuring – would decline and therefore their loans would be at risk. There was no basis for this claim on the part of the Federal Housing Administration.

There were separate housing projects specifically aimed at black people, strategically located to keep whites and blacks in completely different neighborhoods. White Americans were subsidized by the government to move their families from crowded urban centers to the brand-new outlying suburbs. African Americans were given no such deal; this led to a demographic pattern that persists to this day.

The segregation persisted during the Second World War, when veterans were given special privileges when it came to mortgages and homeownership taxes. Though black veterans were technically able to apply for special housing, the pre-existing whites-only fine print meant they would automatically be turned down. The Fair Housing Act would not be in place until 1968, when most African Americans could no longer afford to buy homes in the affluent suburbs.

Racial profiling aside, the New Deal funds helped Chicago weather the Great Depression in better shape than most industrial cities. What got the city – and the country – out of the economic depression was the Second World War.

Chicago was a hotbed of political debate concerning whether or not the United States should join the Allied Forces in Europe, but before the question could be settled, Japanese forces attacked Pearl Harbor in Florida. America joined the war effort and Chicago was one of its primary manufacturers.

Tens of thousands of jobs opened up immediately following the call to war; African Americans, white laborers, and Japanese Americans recently released from wartime detention centers flocked to Chicago in search of employment. In manufacturing aircraft, food rations, parachutes, engines, and dozens of essential military supplies, Chicagoans ensured not only the success of their fellow Americans' forces, but the economic recovery of their country.

Chapter 12 – Century of Progress

"Science Finds, Industry Applies, Man Adapts."

Chicago celebrated its centennial in 1933 and 1934 by hosting another World's Fair. Originally planned to run from May to November of 1933, the event proved so successful that it ran again for six months the following year. The World's Fair: Century of Progress was designed to celebrate how far the city had come since its incorporation and showcase a glimpse into a machine-filled, luxurious future.

Image Source[xxiii]

At the time, the country was waist-deep in the financial turmoil of the Great Depression. Planned before President Roosevelt's New Deal gave Mayor Edward Kelly and Chicago extra funds for social programs and events, the fair was paid for in part with a $10 million bond purchased the day before the crash. By the time the fair closed for good, the entire debt had been repaid. The bulk of the cost (as much as $100 million) was secured by Rufus Dawes. In exchange, Dawes was given heavy input into the theme of the event, as well as its organization.

Some of the burden was taken on by corporations who were invited to take part in the fair with their very own exhibition buildings. Among other branded features were a General Motors Building and a Sears Pavilion.

A team of local architects, led by Paul Cret and Raymond Hood, was assembled to design the pavilion and exhibits. The team, which included Edward Bennet and Hubert Burnham, is said to have overlooked the obvious choice of Frank Lloyd Wright because he was a terrible team player. All the same, Wright had a hand in concept design.

The Century of Progress exhibition was set up in Chicago's nearby Lakefront Northerly Island peninsula. The strip of land was manmade, but at the time was not technically part of the city of Chicago. As Illinois-owned land, Northerly Island offered architects and designers the unique opportunity to create structures that would not have followed Chicago's building code. These were incredibly inventive for the time, as architects used many new, man-made materials such as prefabricated sheetrock, Masonite, and Maizewood. They also incorporated Douglas fir 5-ply and corrugated metal. In terms of modernist shapes, builders were able to construct the first catenary roof (a dome-like structure) ever used in the U.S. atop the Travel and Transport Building. The Brook Hill Farm Dairy features a multi-vaulted ceiling constructed with thin-shell concrete – another American first.

Where the 1893 Columbian Exposition had incorporated classic architecture into its buildings and spatial design, the Century of Progress pavilions would be constructed from modernist plans that had never been seen before. Not only did the fairgrounds include the Hall of Science, a Travel and Transport Building, Horticultural Building, and the infamous House of Tomorrow, but a Lilliputian City of little people and real babies in incubators.

The Houses of Tomorrow are probably one of the best-remembered exhibitions from the Century of Progress fair. These futuristic model homes captured the imaginations of nearly 40 million ticket-holders in 1933 and 1934 and have since turned up time and again in contemporary art and entertainment. They are synonymous with the 1933 Chicago World's Fair, just as the fair itself is synonymous with a positive, hopeful, and quirky portrayal of the future times in which we live today. The energy and memories of those two years have been carried on in American culture, sometimes in unexpected ways.

Image Source[xxiv]

Ray Bradbury wrote a creepy tale called "There Will Come Soft Rains" about a modern home that was entirely computer-controlled. On the lighter side of things, the World's Fair and its popular exhibition have also been memorialized by numerous writers such as Clare Blank, Roy J. Snell, Max Allan Collins, and Jean Shepherd.

There were several model homes exhibited at the fair, one of which bore the superior title "House of Tomorrow." Chicago architect

George Fred Keck designed this house. The structure was 12-sided and 3 stories tall. The top two stories were made of glass, while the first floor featured a little personal airplane hangar. A dishwasher was built into the kitchen, and the home featured air conditioning. In an attempt to prove critics of his design wrong, Keck installed a heating system that allowed solar heat to gather within the house during the winter. Unfortunately, the heating system worked too well in the summer, causing the air conditioning unit to fail.

Five of the model homes, including the House of Tomorrow, were bought by Robert Bartlett and shipped over Lake Michigan to their new home in Indiana. In 2013, the House of Tomorrow was declared a national landmark by the National Trust for Historic Preservation, meaning that it could undergo renovations and repairs. It and the other model homes originally moved by Bartlett are available to tour, though the glass walls of the octagonal-home have been replaced for better air flow.

President Roosevelt himself requested that the Century of Progress continue for a second year. In the midst of the Depression, he was impressed by the influence the event had on the average American, who still had an income and a place to live. Roosevelt wanted those people to continue spending so that the gears of the American economy could speed up once again; it was a tactic that worked, and corporations that had declined participation in the 1933 schedule fell over themselves to get a spot in the 1934 run. Among the second-year newcomers was the Ford Motor Company, eager to outshine the popular General Motors' assembly-line exhibition.

Not everything went according to plan at the fair. During the first year, as many as 1,400 people became seriously sick after attending. An investigation was carried out and it was discovered that every case of amoebic dysentery could be traced back to two hotels. The food was tested, but soon it became evident that the hotels shared a contaminated plumbing system in which the sewer lines were leaking into the fresh water pipes. The problem was solved and the fair moved on, but at least 98 people died that year.

The World's Fair Century of Progress made a lasting impression on Chicago and the rest of the United States, and indeed the world. Six years later, New York hosted another World's Fair, dubbed the World of Tomorrow with a clear nod to the earlier Chicago event.

The Chicago city flag, originally designed with two six-pointed red stars between two horizontal blue stripes over a white background, was altered in reverence to the Century of Progress. The first star is for Fort Dearborn, a military outpost that preceded heavy settlement in Chicago. The second star is symbolic of the Great Chicago Fire of 1871. The third and fourth stars represent the 1893 Columbian Exposition and the World's Fair Century of Progress.

Chapter 13 – The Pinkerton National Detective Agency

The Pinkertons have been one of Chicago's most influential and long-lasting organizations, and it all started when a Scottish man named Allan Pinkerton immigrated to an area outside the city in 1842. He found a job-making barrels but within five years had joined the Chicago Police Department. After several years with the police, Pinkerton was made a detective. He opened his own agency in the 1850s, and the Pinkerton National Detective Agency was born. It stood at 80 Washington Street.

Image Source[xxv]

Pinkerton's first big case outside of the police department involved protecting dead bodies in Chicago's cemetery. At the time, there was an underground market for cadavers that medical schools could study and research. Very few dead bodies for the medical field were legally provided, but doctors and scientists were just starting to uncover the hidden secrets of the human body and they weren't prepared to stop. People who supplied extra cadavers were known as Resurrectionists.

In the 1850s, Chicago's dead fell prey to the Resurrectionist trade. When four fresh graves were found empty, detectives moved on the area and staked it out for several days. After days of no action, they spotted a buggy pulling away from the cemetery one night, containing two cadavers and Martin Quinlan, the city Sexton. The man was fined $500 after appearing in court.

The grave robbery case made Pinkerton famous in Chicago, but he found national fame when he discovered and prevented a plot to assassinate President-elect Abraham Lincoln on the way to his inauguration. It was called the Baltimore Plot. According to Lincoln's private secretary, **John Nicolay**, the soon-to-be President had a number of enemies:

> His mail was infested with brutal and vulgar menace, and warnings of all sorts came to him from zealous or nervous friends. But he had himself so sane a mind, and a heart so kindly, even to his enemies, that it was hard for him to believe in political hatred so deadly as to lead to murder.

Nicolay was concerned over the upcoming rail trip to Washington, as was railway executive Samuel Morse Felton. Upon hearing rumors that anti-Union conspirators were planning to besiege his trains, Felton hired the most famous detective he'd heard of: Allen Pinkerton. The detective reportedly set off to meet Felton the moment he read the man's letter.

Though Felton and Pinkerton were equally worried about the upcoming inauguration, it hadn't occurred to either of them that

Lincoln's life was in danger. When they discovered an assassination plot awaiting the President-elect in Baltimore, the detective had Lincoln travel through the city secretly, moving on to Washington at the back of the train - in disguise.

Said Pinkerton: "Vice may triumph for a time, crime may flaunt its victories in the face of honest toilers, but in the end the law will follow the wrong-doer to a bitter fate, and dishonor and punishment will be the portion of those who sin."

Following the successful train journey and inauguration, Lincoln hired Pinkerton's agency to look after him during the Civil War. In 1871, Congress' Department of Justice budget ran low, and so internal investigations were outsourced to the Pinkerton Detective Agency. By 1893, this was found to be a conflict of interest that led to the Anti-Pinkerton Act. Nevertheless, the agency played a vital role in the protection of America's business and political interests in the nineteenth century.

One of the agents on the Baltimore Plot case was Kate Warne, the first female detective in the United States. She was a national treasure, described by Pinkerton himself in an 1883 book called The Spy of the Rebellion as:

> [A] commanding person, with clear-cut, expressive features...a slender, brown-haired woman, graceful in her movements and self-possessed. Her features, although not what could be called handsome [beautiful], were decidedly of an intellectual cast... her face was honest, which would cause one in distress instinctly [sic] to select her as a confidante.

Pinkerton was surprised when Warne entered his office in Chicago and expressed her interest in becoming a detective. He told her as much, but she argued that a woman would be privy to conversations and situations that men could not so easily access. She won over the boss and was hired, soon proving herself as the star detective in a case against an embezzler with the Adams Express Company. In

1860, Pinkerton created a female detective agency and put Kate Warne in charge.

The Pinkerton detectives cultivated an excellent reputation with businesses and government, but the organization also did its best to stay on good terms with the citizens they were protecting. In the years following the Civil War, America's soldiers, freed slaves, and displaced workers found themselves in troubled times. Thousands of them had no recourse except to walk or ride the rails from city to city, looking for work or a hand-out. Middle-class and wealthy people were afraid to come across such people, and they reached out to the police and local detectives like Pinkerton for protection from the perceived threat. The head of the agency kept his cool when it came to the situation, taking pity instead of making undue arrests:

> What other recourse have these people had save to turn tramp, and beg and pilfer to sustain life? It is a pitiable condition of things, but there is no doubt that the majority of those now upon the road are there from necessity, and not from choice. If thousands are here from abroad who have been compelled to turn tramp, how many of our own people have been forced into the same kind of life as the only way left to live outside of the poor-house?

Today, there are Pinkerton offices all across the United States and the rest of the world; the company specializes in risk management and security. There is still a Pinkerton branch in Chicago, and Kate Warne is buried in the Pinkerton family plot in the city's Graceland Cemetery.

Chapter 14 – The Daley Dynasty

Since the early nineteenth century, Chicago has been home to a robust Irish immigrant population. The city's Irish-Americans have been a driving force in the workplace, as well as some of the most prominent union leaders throughout history. In 1955, Richard J. Daley, an Irish-descended citizen of Chicago, became the city's mayor. He would stay in office until his death in 1975, having served his city for 21 years.

Image Source[xxvi]

Under Daley's leadership, Chicago's O'Hare International Airport was constructed to replace the undersized Midway Airport. The features of O'Hare really set it apart from the world's existing airports at the time, including the underground refueling system and direct terminal access from the highway. It was built for the future, and Daley was admittedly very proud of it. O'Hare was the world's busiest airport from 1963 to 1998, and during the Cold War it was an active fighter base.

Daley's time in the mayoral office was not without its turmoil. In fact, several members of his political administration were charged and convicted of corruption. But those two decades were vital in terms of cultural and ethnic evolution. Chicago was home to large ethnic minority groups, including Irish, German, Polish, Italian and African Americans, and yet most of these groups were segregated from middle and upper-class whites in terms of jobs, wages and physical neighborhoods. The New Deal housing policies from the 1930s were still in place. Even Daley himself lived in Bridgeport, a notoriously Irish part of the city.

In 1966, Martin Luther King, Jr. and James Bevel of the Southern Christian Leadership Conference visited Chicago to kick-off civil rights activism in the city. Mayor Daley decided to meet with the two men in a summit conference and signed a pledge promising to work toward fair and open housing. Since the pledge wasn't based in actual legislation, it didn't accomplish much. When King was murdered in 1968, President Lyndon B. Johnson signed the Fair Housing Act into law.

Mayor Daley was harshly criticized for his words following the civil rights activist's murder. When the public found out about King's death, riots broke out across the United States, with Chicago, Baltimore, and Washington D.C. experiencing the worst of it. Discussing a conversation he'd had with police superintendent James B. Conlisk, Daley told the press, "I said to him very emphatically and very definitely that an order be issued by him immediately to shoot to kill any arsonist or anyone with a Molotov cocktail in his hand, because they're potential murderers, and to shoot to maim or cripple anyone looting."

After receiving backlash for his heavy-handed approach to the dissidence, Daley retracted his earlier statement: "It is the established policy of the police department – fully supported by this administration – that only the minimum force necessary be used by policemen in carrying out their duties." Later that month, Daley asserted, "There wasn't any shoot-to-kill order. That was a fabrication."

Things didn't get any easier for Mayor Daley that year. In addition to Martin Luther King, Robert Kennedy had been murdered while running for president. Later, in the midst of the Vietnam War, the United States was also split on whether to stay the course or send troops home. When the Democratic Convention came to Chicago that year, the public took it as an opportunity to voice their concerns. More rioting occurred during the convention, with police stepping in and things turning violent. Daley defended the actions of his police force, and in 1971, he was re-elected for the fifth and final time.

After Daley's death, Michael Anthony Bilandic took over as mayor until 1979. A decade later, Richard M. Daley was elected; he would serve one year more than his famous father had.

The industrial machines of the western world were as strong as ever in the 1950s and 1960s, when the first Daley came to power. By the 1980s, however, the so-called Rust Belt of America had started to form, stretching from New York to Wisconsin. America – and Chicago – was losing industrial and manufacturing jobs to China and Japan, who could produce for less money. Mayor Richard M. Daley could let his city sink into another economic depression, or he could find a way to spark a new economic era. He chose the latter. According to the *Chicago Sun-Times*:

> Daley took over control of the public schools when more timid politicians urged caution. He embraced the Chicago Housing Authority, promising better homes and better lives for residents,

knowing there would be political fallout and it was sure to hurt him. He built Millennium Park, brought life and theater back to the Loop at night, created the Museum Campus, made city beautification a top priority and went after O'Hare expansion. He has taken bold action and big risks when he safely could have settled for less, pushing Chicago forward and securing its future.

Chapter 15 – Oprah Winfrey and Harpo

Chicago has been home to many great men and women, but one of those stands out to a generation of African Americans and women: Oprah Winfrey. Not only has her international success story inspired millions, but Winfrey's production company, Harpo, provided jobs, entertainment and a source of pride for Chicago for over two decades. Hers is a story of entrepreneurship and overcoming obstacles that gives hope to many Americans, most of whom will always relate the name Oprah Winfrey to the city of Chicago.

Image Source[xxvii]

Oprah's story began the way many others in poverty-stricken American did. She was born to a teenage mother in Mississippi, poor and underprivileged due to circumstance and race. The 1950s were still harsh times in America for African Americans, particularly those without a strong family unit and financial stability. After becoming pregnant and losing her unborn son at the age of 14, the young girl went to Tennessee to live with the man who (correctly or not) was named as her father on her 1954 birth certificate.

That's where Oprah's story stops being commonplace because as a young teenager, she began to really focus on making a life for herself. Winfrey picked up a job while still in high school, working at a local all-black radio station. By the time she was nineteen years old, she was co-hosting the local evening news. She moved on to television newscasting in Baltimore and Nashville before finding the job that would land her smack-dab in the middle of the daytime talk show arena in Chicago.

Talk shows were just coming into their own when Oprah was tasked with improving the ratings of a television show called AM Chicago. It was 1984, and Winfrey was breaking all kinds of broadcasting rules in an industry that was largely white and male-centric. That first show didn't go too well - in Oprah's own words, "Everything went wrong. I was cooking, and I don't cook."

Oprah's on-screen personality won the audience over, and within a month, AM Chicago was top-rated in its home city. The next year, she was nominated for an Academy Award for Best Supporting Actress for her role as Sofia in Steven Spielberg's *The Color Purple*, and her skyrocketing popularity inspired the WLS-TV station to rebrand her morning show. Beginning in 1986, the poor girl from Mississippi found herself hosting *The Oprah Winfrey Show*.

The show ran for a total of 25 seasons, broadcasting its final episode in May of 2011. During that time, Oprah started her own production company, Harpo Productions, becoming the producer of her own show. She launched branded magazines and created the Oprah Winfrey Network (OWN). She starred in the movie *Beloved*, in which she played a former slave struggling with her past – and a haunted house. During the show itself, Oprah became known for gifting every single audience member with amazing prizes, including a trip to Disneyland and a brand-new car.

Even after *The Oprah Winfrey Show* was finished, Oprah's various projects and companies employed more than 12,500 people, most of them situated in Chicago. She was – and is – an industry unto herself. In becoming the wealthiest African American woman in history, Oprah was always focused on giving back to the people and the city that had supported her.

Only the Internal Revenue Service truly knows the amount of money Oprah has spent on charities near and far, but even without a full tally it's clear that she'd dedicated millions of dollars to Chicagoans, Americans, and the international community. According to Inside Philanthropy, "The bulk of Winfrey's giving has gone to educational causes, including charter schools, programs that support African-American students, and the Oprah Winfrey Leadership Academy in South Africa."

Hundreds of thousands of Oprah's charitable dollars have been directed at educational facilities, with particular focus on improving educational opportunities for African American students in America and abroad. She founded the Oprah Winfrey Leadership Academy for Girls in South Africa, a school for which she handpicks students who have often been abused multiple times or suffered the loss of family members.

At home in Chicago, Winfrey saw another chance to help underprivileged students at the Providence St. Mel School on the West Side. With roots going back as far as the Stock Market Crash, St. Mel School was transformed in the 1970s under the leadership of Principal Paul J. Adams. Adams created a strict regime at the school whereby no student was permitted to participate in gang-related behavior, fight on school grounds, or engage in illegal activities like stealing or using drugs. Punishment for any such behavior was expulsion.

Soon after the school's new identity, the Catholic ruling body decided to shut it down. Principal Adams fought to keep it open, which resulted in its independent status as a college preparatory facility. Eventually, it expanded to accept students from pre-kindergarten age to grade 12. Since the 1970s, St. Mel School boasts that every single graduating student has been accepted to college. The school is considered a cornerstone of Chicago's educational system, but there have been many times it faced financial difficulties. In 1993, Oprah Winfrey gave Providence St. Mel School $1 million.

The African American female powerhouse of America's "Second City" has also contributed to Habitat for Humanity, Save the Children, the International Brain Research Foundation, Smithsonian's National Museum of African American History and Culture, the National Council of Negro Women, and Green Belt International, and given $1 million to Chicago's Millennium Park.

In 2017, Oprah's visage was painted into a mural on the Chicago Cultural Center alongside other pioneering Chicago personalities like Barbara Gaines (founder and artistic director of Chicago Shakespeare Theater) and Susanne Ghez of the Renaissance Society.

Said Kerry James Marshall, the artist, "Given it's the Cultural Center and its role in the city, it made perfect sense to honor these women who've been important to cultural life in so many institutions."

Winfrey has since relocated to Montecito, California, but her empire continues to employ and inspire people in Chicago and the rest of the United States. She remains a cultural icon and role model for African Americans, Chicagoans, women, and underprivileged black students everywhere.

Chapter 16 – Chicago Today

Modern Chicago is everything the last two hundred years have made it: a skyscraper skyline, repurposed factories housing people, and Generation-Y startups. Mid-century family homes and modernist apartments. A population of immigrant-descendants with pride in their history and hope for their children's children. It's a city that is always on the precipice of the future, whether it likes it or not.

Contemporary Chicago is a city of more than 2 million people, many of whom have genuine beliefs about the correct thickness of a pizza crust, and strict ideas about hot dog toppings. These same people bike through the greenery of Millennium Park or strap on a pair of ice skates to visit the rink at the center of it. They take their kids to the Navy Pier for ice cream and carnival rides. And chances are, they work in the healthcare industry or service sector.

Right now, Chicago's economy is speeding alongside the best of them, adapting to new technology and consumer demands in real-time. It doesn't matter whether beaver pelts, steel beams, or talk shows are the next big thing in the world marketplace, Chicago will find a way to make it and sell it. These days, that innovative spirit is largely at work in medical offices, hospitals, food service, hospitality, and government support offices.

Chicago's multiculturalism is still at the forefront of its identity, though the scars of racial and cultural inequality can still be seen in non-diverse housing areas and ongoing tension between races. Nevertheless, more African American families have begun moving from heavy urban downtown areas and into Chicago's suburbs.

As the struggle for racial equality forges onward, Chicago holds claim to the most popular U.S. President in recent history: Barack Hussein Obama. Born in Hawaii, Obama lived in Seattle, Indonesia, New York, and eventually Chicago. He served in the Illinois Senate from 1997 to 2004 before being elected to the U.S. Senate. He served in the latter until 2008, when he was elected President.

Image Source[xxviii]

Barack married Michelle in 1992, and the couple lived in Chicago with their growing family until the new President was called to the White House. For African Americans in Chicago, the prestige of sharing their city with an educated, accomplished black person who went on to lead the entire country was unprecedented. Senator and then President Obama represented everything that an African American should be able to accomplish in the modern America. Chicago voted overwhelmingly for the Democrats in both of Obama's presidential campaigns, winning the president 20 electoral votes for Illinois.

After his time in the White House came to an end, Barack Obama gave his hometown an official farewell:

> So I first came to Chicago when I was in my early twenties, and I was still trying to figure out who I was; still searching for a

purpose to my life. And it was a neighborhood not far from here where I began working with church groups in the shadows of closed steel mills. It was on these streets where I witnessed the power of faith, and the quiet dignity of working people in the face of struggle and loss.

Later on, amid swarms of supporters *and* protesters – perhaps the hallmark of any major undertaking in Chicago – the city hosted a conference concerning the proposed Obama Presidential Center on the South Side. Ultimately green-lighted by the Chicago City Council, the project is moving forward. The Obama Presidential Center will be a public Presidential library, one that the former President's organization claims will provide 5,000 jobs during construction, and 2,500 jobs for continued administration and maintenance. Obama has made it clear that he wants to give back to Chicago for all the years he spent there raising a family and starting his political career. His foundation has received thousands of letters and postcards asking for the library to be built, and specifically on the classically impoverished South Side.

As it always has, Chicago embraces tomorrow with an expectation of hard work, but the hope of satisfying payoff. It demands the best and strives toward that goal. As Mike Royko, Chicago columnist, once said, "One of the hallmarks of Chicago is that we do so many things in an original manner. What other city has made a river flow backward? What other city makes traffic flow backward?"

Check out this book!

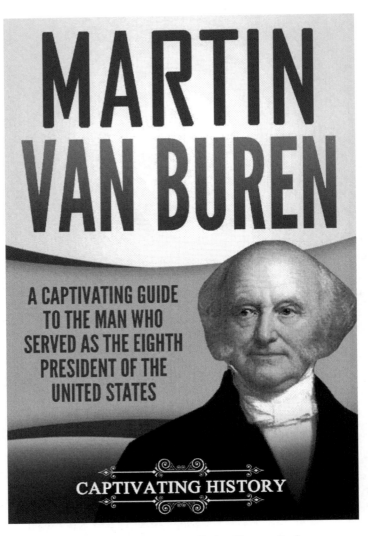

Check out this book!

Check out this book!

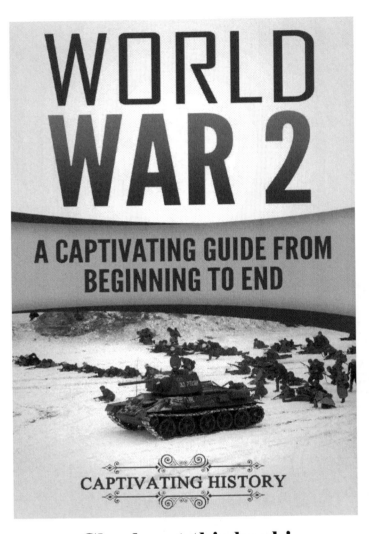

Check out this book!

Notes on Images

[i] *Picture from Xasartha, Wikimedia Commons*
[ii] *Photo by Teemu008, Wikimedia Commons*
[iii] *Photo by Railsr4me, Flickr*
[iv] *Public Domain Photo from 1890*
[v] *Photo from Rand, McNally & Co, Wikimedia Commons*
[vi] *Photo from Rand, McNally & Co, Wikimedia Commons*
[vii] *Photo by MindFrieze, Flickr*
[viii] *Photo by Erica Schoonmaker, Flickr*
[ix] *Photo by David Wilson, Flickr*
[x] *Photo from Anne Rossley, Flickr*
[xi] *Photo from Chicago Architecture Today, Flickr*
[xii] *Photo by E. Benjamin Andrews, Public Domain*
[xiii] *Photo from TonyTheTiger at Wikipedia*
[xiv] *Photo from National Park Service, Flickr*
[xv] *Photo from C. D. Arnold (1844-1927); H. D. Higinbotham, Wikimedia Commons*
[xvi] *Photo from Boston Public Library, Flickr*
[xvii] *Photo from United States Bureau of Prisons, Wikimedia Commons*
[xviii] *Photo from Lou Stejskal, Flickr*
[xix] *Photo from Discover DuPage, Flickr*
[xx] *Photo from The DLC, Flickr*
[xxi] *Photo from Bryan... at Flickr*
[xxii] *Photo from dandeluca, Flickr*
[xxiii] *Public Domain Photo*
[xxiv] *Photo by Chris Light, Wikimedia Commons*
[xxv] *Photo from Library of Congress Prints and Photographs Division, Wikimedia Commons*
[xxvi] *Photo from U.S. News & World Report, Wikimedia Commons*
[xxvii] *Photo from aphrodite_in_nyc, Flickr*
[xxviii] *Photo by Pete Souza*

Free Bonus from Captivating History (Available for a Limited time)

Hi History Lovers!

Now you have a chance to join our exclusive history list so you can get your first history ebook for free as well as discounts and a potential to get more history books for free! Simply visit the link below to join.

Captivatinghistory.com/ebook

Also, make sure to follow us on:

Twitter: @Captivhistory

Facebook: Captivating History:@captivatinghistory